Unearthly Toys

Ned Denny was born in London in 1975. He has worked as a postman, art critic, book reviewer, music journalist, and gardener. His poems and masks have appeared in publications including *PN Review*, *Poetry Review*, *The White Review*, *Oxford Poetry*, *The Times Literary Supplement*, and *Modern Poetry in Translation*.

to those who swim against the tide
*

and in loving memory of my father

UNEARTHLY TOYS

POEMS AND MASKS

NED DENNY

CARCANET

First published in Great Britain in 2018 by
CARCANET PRESS Ltd
Alliance House, 30 Cross Street
Manchester M2 7AQ

A CIP catalogue record for this book is available
from the British Library: ISBN 9781784105389

Design: Luke Allan.
Printed and bound in England by SRP Ltd.

The publisher acknowledges financial assistance
from Arts Council England.

After having searched the heights and pastures without having found that panther which we are pursuing, let us now track her in a more rational manner, in order that we may, through diligent study, trap in our snares she who is everywhere fragrant but nowhere seen.

DANTE, *De Vulgari Eloquentia*

...I have been a tree amid the wood
And many a new thing understood
That was rank folly to my head before.

EZRA POUND, *The Tree*

I would like to thank my grandfather Norman Reid – for the volumes of Blake and Pound, where it began; Brian Patten, Seamus Heaney and Simon Armitage – the ones who wrote back; Eric Griffiths – who saw something in me; Michael Schmidt – for several years of kindly responses, and the subsequent support; Ed Clarke – for the correspondence, the encouragement, and the synchronicities; and, finally, those I have no need to name – you know who you are.

CONTENTS

So who's it for, this monumental book
finessed with the pumice stone of my hard head?

For you, *the only one able to look
deep within my ravings for a kind of sense,*

*and who once, in a dream, dared to unfold
the world's slow reversion to iron from gold:*

*a feat of graft and sheer intellection.
Here, wisest friend, it's all yours if you can lift*

*it or hold it down. Dear girl, God's sweet gift,
may it last longer than the review section!*

1

House Music

HOUSE MUSIC

Consider the architecture of the fire,
this radiant palace receiving in turn
the great bare mouth of the smallest creature
and the mirrored, steel-cored tower
of your pride; consider that soon
that grim ember

resembling the face we all fear or desire
will be the perch where you sing and do not burn,
peace be within thee, vigilant preacher
of the mind-consuming hour
each undergoes and what the moon
must dismember;

and consider while these agile days climb higher,
witchlike as flame – as the stuttering intern
is fanned to a tall and brilliant teacher –
how to step into that power,
that breathing room, the killer tune
you'll remember.

WHO'S SHE

after Arnaut Daniel

Sweet precision
of the mind-manifesting
voice of the birds, the luminous argot
blown from tree to tree just as we implore
those whom love makes us see more and less clearly,
you inspire me – whose perverted soul sways true,
straight in its windings – to conceive the finest
call, a chirp with no bum note or word astray.

Indecision,
that luxury! No dithering
could touch me when I first breached the snow
of her smooth ramparts, the girl I thirst for
with a wild intensity that is nearly
unendurable, the shining one, she who
has hands whose omniscience exceeds the rest
as surely as love's gentlest caress bests a

circumcision.
She clocked me, my discerning
between the real deal and the fake – *we* know
how true gold's hidden by the lead uproar
of our toys – and as our tongues moved sincerely
she drew her dark cloak of constellated blue
so the boys that speak in the snake's interest
couldn't leer at what all babble fails to say.

No spring vision
(birds interpret as they sing)
of flowers limning the unguarded flow
of heaven is fresher; without her, *L'Or*
gives skin no glow nor JPMorgan's yearly

profits; within her high castle's living pew
our seeming leaders might be less possessed,
all who exchange her presence for the Devil's pay.

God's elision
in life's book of our killing –
that only sin – our joy with our sorrow
surely bodes well for his setting some store
by holy communion, wherein we'll merely
look and kiss and laugh along each bared sinew
as I measure the lovely weight of a breast
where the light, the embodied light, swells its ray.

Ah, derision
for my own solemn honking
bites once more – sound in which we think we go
about the gardens of an emperor,
dreamt court in which we whisper cavalierly
as his money man – and I'd be a fool to
mouth her name and put love to the test:
no saint protects those whose chatter keeps the dawn at bay.

RIP

You are just about to turn for home,
back to the chickens strutting in the dirt
and village gossip and a tonguelash from her,

when something in the silence holds you.
It is a quiet composed of many sounds
(each one as small as it is clear)

that call and call to a distant stillness
our dialect has no words for.
You fall to the grass. The hour's a song

to empty the skull, moving in the giant sky
and men disguised as mountain pines.
It is as though you have been asleep,

as if you have stumbled out of time.
The dwarves are gone. Their dreamless faces
leer from the rocks and the rocky clouds,

down at the trees whose ascent is music.
You are just about to turn for home.
The minutes pass like seasons, centuries.

HMP WANDSWORTH

Down the rain-sweetened paths of the garden centre
an old boy handles a broom like a dancer, sweeps
with an unhurried grace that is almost tender
or stoops to pick up the eaten face of a rose,
a toppled plant. Such is the knowledge manifest
in gesture, the genius of fingers, as this wild

day makes an avenue of lindens plunge like wild
horses, as someone who moves from his deep centre
makes the body's divinity manifestly
clear. Past a fence and a road, the arrested sweep
of HM's broken clock speaks volumes, conjures rows
of locked sky-blue doors and the illegal tender

of phones and weed in those walls where none are tender,
then the gent who spat in the face of Oscar Wilde
at Clapham Junction station, the tears he claimed rose
that hour each day, and all horrors heaven-sent, a
black wind from the sun that will scour our bones and sweep
us to the end where Love, for ever, manifests.

I have taken a pinch of mind-manifester
(though 'spirit-' surely gets it better), more tender
with each dismantling minute, rudderless, swept
by my breath across a common newly-wild
to glare at the glaring brick of the Visitors' Centre,
to gaze at unearthly cars muscular in rows

and glimpse in tinted glass my face's cankered rose.
At Neal's Nurseries, plants are checked on manifests;
I lope by and think of you, miscreant scenter
of what life might be if we could remain tender,
flower-child, dark beholder, prophet of the wild
presence that lives unseen in the woodland's poised sweep,

of flesh as soul. The wind is at large. Horned clouds sweep
over alleys of grey-green, exultant rock rose.
In a tone wildly calm as it is calmly wild
the rhododendron reprints its manifesto –
with a verve so unlike all wordy pretenders! –
at each outspread upper petal's silk-cool centre

and an ambulance sweeps down the road's dead centre,
blue roses keening. Turning, that tender
man flashes me a wild smile. Holy ghosts remanifest.

LOGOS
after Baudelaire

As a child I woke in a book-illumined room
where all possible genres spoke, a soundless blare
of deviant science, art, the myths of Tahiti;
I was about the height of a slim volume.

Two voices possessed me. A silken one feigned care:
This cut-price world's more sweet than a fondant fancy,
and I'll give you an appetite deep as a tomb
to shove it in. The other was a kind of prayer,

a mere breath. *Come,* it said, *come! Your dreaming's a sea*
whose dark riptides are flowering, a flowing loom
where the unknown's woven, and it sang like the air
on the shore, the serpentine air, the air that we

feel flicker at the ear's meat like its jewelled doom.
I answered with a Yes, and it was there
and then my head was opened, my fatality
fixed as the one who sees the realms inhabiting the gloom

that revolves the stars and upholds each stair,
the worlds behind this vast theatre's flimsy scenery;
I sense the snakes curled on our shoes and costume,
ecstatic victim of the fact that my *voyance* is *clair*.

Since then, too, like the giants of prophecy,
I love the rolling desert light, the sea's dry boom,
and weep when others cheer and laugh at despair
and even find a savour in the 'W' and 'B',

and see that so-called truths are not as we assume
whilst falling down a hole with my interstellar stare.
No matter, I have my voice and it consoles me:
a wise man's dreams are built but a fool's dreams bloom.

THREE OLD SONGS

i

Yet once more, the plum tree is transfigured;
the birds recite their Angelus again.
Discomforted by the odd green flame,
he douses the patio with weed-killer.

ii

The black widow's hourglass hangs in our windows.
In our porches, the beetles stroll at their ease.

Dream-weather escalates: tremors, tornados.
Instead of a fire, the cold blaze of a screen

casts blue glimmerings through palatial dark.
Intelligent talk drowns out an exile's scream;

gates with rust-spotted padlocks keep us from parks
where the sunlight moves from seed to golden seed.

iii

Observe the elusive nature of the goddess:
she is nowhere to be seen in your languages,
but on your vision's periphery, the garden's
every leaf is exultant with her presence.

AFTER CAVALCANTI

Loveliness of women and what the heart knows
the ineffable charm a loaded gun has
love's rationale the blackbird's 3 a.m. jazz
expertise of white ships when death's current flows
the sheer unruffled silentness of the snow's
windless descent dawn air before day's business
silver and gold and the *lapis exilis*
a stream's clear sinew bee orchids in meadows

these things are fine but my darling surpasses
their beauties with a quiet soul that knows no fear
and makes all men who see her feel just *so* tall

her innate understanding and wisdom is
as remote and as rare as the troposphere
to want to be with her is only natural

GRISLIE

This waterway is of the first water.
This is the art of water torture.
I am the water boatman, dancer on waters,
patroller of a flowing border.

They're led here at nightfall like horses to water.
They expect watermelons, water-ice,
a watercolour sky, cups and saucers.
My pitilessness is watertight.

I offer water biscuits, limes to suck.
A man offers up a baby daughter.
Their noisy grief slips off me like water off a duck.
They know they cannot walk on water.

ENGRAVED (COME TO DADDY)

To be pinned beneath a ceiling that is beaming
to see that flesh is subatomic gnomes going whee
the pythagorean perfection of the woods
blessed are the undefiled in the way
a diorite craft a white stag flying blind
digital bushbabies their faces poised
on the precise midpoint between joy and horror
and in the mist of tears and under running laughter
the wild boar in the embers of your mind

and I imagined you had rolled into the fire
burning as you slept but I could not cry aloud
and the queen chanting backwards in cabalistic code
from thought to thought from hill to hill love doth me lead
the pausing sidewinding and flowering of time
what red riding hood encountered on the path
yea though thou diest I say I shall not die
a praying mantis shaking you awake
where there is danger there grows also what saves

the goat's face reminding you of something you'll forget
the wolf who is standing on the end of the bed
the spreading tree of your polar blood
trembling in the wind from a blue-toned star
(men have not language to describe
one moment of your eternal life)
and that tall tale of how he saw or thought he saw
the wrestler gorgeous george mouth
you're making it come alive

one who knows how to keep silent in words
the crone and her otters on the roof of the cathedral
following the vision that our minds have seen
and the masks that they wear and the games that they play

and sleep on tap and the bushes full of witches
here at the great centre-stone of earth's broad breast
good morning mister dragon good morning mister dragon
with void mouth gape after emptier prey
a dazzling pinecone implanted in the brain

predynastic devices a people of strange language
a number too immense for all creation to contain
and they said to one another behold this dreamer cometh
the arcanum of daylight and the leaping buds
each and every one of them a right little terror
and an aged voice that calls from inside the hill
oh kings oh kings you are diligent lackeys
the inexorable approach of the drumming mice
the dungeon master's fatal error

2

Ventriloquise

FIR

after Bernart de Ventadorn

When you see the sun-made lark's wings whirr
against the counterpressure of that light
and slow until a hypersonic stillness
has him drop, a stone shaped like a heart,
it's as though you step into a green rain
of envy of those whose smile is no disguise,
wondering that your chest's flagrance
isn't instantly reduced to a spent black wick.

You thought you got love but your thoughts were
simulacra, a counterfeit delight,
for what idea can cage the pace of the kiss
you pursue in dreams and trace in art;
she has stolen your blood's loving refrain,
nabbed her sweet self, has purloined the very skies
and in so doing's left a dunce
caressing thin air to the soundtrack of a tick.

You're no longer the fat controller
of yourself, squinting from a tourist's height,
since you glanced into those eyes where all joy is;
as mirrors hold death and life apart
they disclosed your second self, free of pain
as a meat suit is nipped at by shoals of sighs;
you're shut out from your days, as once
Narcissus was undone by his own biopic.

You'd wash your hands of her and all her
kind – whose ways are at ease, whose touch is light –
vowing that just as you once sang her wholeness
now your branching tongue shall flick and dart,
seeing how they close their ranks and disdain

to aid one who shakes in her dawn air, who dies
into the vast clairaudience
in which each opened tree receives an old magic.

And in such things, alight under fur,
she shows herself to be a dame alright,
not resting content with the bland park that is
permitted by that celestial fart
but reaching for the fruit that fires the brain;
I'm afraid that you're a joke in her bright eyes,
roped to the cliff of appetence
with no companion but the music of your pick.

Grace is gone from the world, you aver,
yet what have you ever known but this night
in which the sainted mother of our riches
has been replaced by a doll, a tart,
a bulb-eyed changeling whose synthetic reign
is the false light, a grim tree, which if you're wise
enough to unspell appearance –
now's the time – you'll know for the shade that makes us sick.

Your tame prayer is just a verbal blur
wholly failing to manifest your 'right'
to her who can be the riskiest mistress –
the cyclone her voice – so why not start
a trilled silence, burn books, begin again;
let death be the force that you ventriloquise,
that end which is the newborn dance
danced in exile by those who are so slain they're quick.

GAZELLE

And let me die before my death!
HENRY VAUGHAN, *REGENERATION*

There are some who insist on voicing the dusk
without first silently drinking the dusk.

A line of bared trees is a line of adepts,
their delicate fingers playing the dusk.

To legislate on the progress of souls!
As preposterous as outlawing the dusk.

The seer who ministers to his people
makes an honest living climbing the dusk.

The loss of their minds was due to the music
heard by the scientists mapping the dusk.

'This water is no right but should be paid for,'
said the CEO, packaging the dusk.

Thought is an ape but the heart's a gazelle
God murders to aid in your feeling the dusk.

When you pack and you ship to your off-world home,
make sure you don't forget to bring the dusk.

The genuine poem as much as a skull
is a living room containing the dusk.

To ease that despotism of the eye,
perhaps it's a matter of *being* the dusk.

A girl with no head is a day-sized bird,
one blue wing the dawn and one blue wing the dusk.

All six hundred and sixty-six channels
simultaneously defaming the dusk.

A soul from afar in miraculous dress,
you have to lose your name to sing the dusk.

ANNUNCIATION

She is attacked one bookish day
for no discernible reason
by a beautifully dressed man.

She admires the velvet collar
of his elegant coat
as he launches himself at her with both hands.

She observes the stitching of his boots
as he kicks her
in the face with all his might.

O he left me kneeling in a garden,
my hands filled with blood
and each dark cell alight.

MAY

birds in immaculate trees
gossiping of God
his outrageous ways

ODE (SEMILANCEATA 312)

in hoc signo vinces

Each one laughs because it is itself all of her, the
real substantial presence of her eternal temper,
ecstatic in an equally serene and raving ease.

Come to me my lost ones and I will make you antic
that long-unwatched song warbles from the bony dust,
not just the whole imagination's manumission

in thistle-starred fields but – feel! – the wrists' virtuosi.
Praise to the lance-snapping folk of the blood, praise the deep
pouring its dark weather on our brains, the Phrygian cap

lifted in snide greeting when the constant moon is full
(each a child of the feral Word, each the freedom pole
seen by leaf-bearded Rip beside the strange-eyed houses

on the dreaming green). Praise to the disordered, those who
find the broadcast wine repugnant as the sluggish loaf,
the ones – *Nature loves courage* – who'll tune to the forest

her science builds, she who unlocks the night with the feath-
er of an owl. Praise her sky-wide incarnation, praise
goddess almighty in the black guise of a dog

or the earthbound earth-transcending tree, praise the holy No
dealt out without regret to the brethren of the dead;
death rends each breath in the empire that's not ended,

except in that unalone apocalyptic peace
subsequent to the sacrament, Sophia's glowing kiss
silencing the virtual serpent's televised hiss.

I bought it because of the backwards 's' and the teeth of the mouth, the jagged lip: DADDIES FAVOURITE ꙅAUCE. He'd unearthed it in the seventies. It cost me a pound or a fiver. 'An error. Unusual. "Under the radar"'. His wink made me think of the interloper, of things renewed, of things reversed. The glass was the clearest, palest blue.

When I handed it over, a bird called from the garden – this is just as it happened, I have it here – and you read it as DAD DIES. That made me cry. That made me wonder.

FAERIE

I sing of Times trans-shifting...

The space between two seconds is our palace,
the fire where we thumb our noses at the world
and chatter in tongues with all the lost boys and girls
(before you were born, you had another face
that the nothing between words mouths back to you
or you glimpse in the darkness between two pines,
the face that can slip in and out of time).
The colours seem brighter, the sky more blue

and the white milk thick when our city alights
in the copse on the outskirts of the village,
when we reappear at the close of an age
to rattle the panes of your double-glazed minds.
The kaleidoscopic head of the bee knows us
and the tree that is dancing yet does not move

and those retuned to the frequency of love.
It is time to say goodbye to the circus,
to come and disport in serious wonder
in the pixellated precincts of our queen.

We are here. Our joy is to trouble your sleep.
The prison falls; the dawn comes up like thunder.

EXILES

after the Old English

The outsiders will be blessed, will move in the ways of the Measurer, though for now they tread with their bare hands the wailing roads of the cities, the just and preordained tarmac of their exile. Or so we tell ourselves, mindful of the unspeakable, the cut-glass tones of the killing machines, the person under the train. Take thought, take thought. How often have we, alone, in the God-charged hour near dawn, lamented with the light lamenters, the callers of His names from tree to shivered tree. But where can we tell of this, who can we show our dreams? Nowhere and no one, for the treasuries of our brains are weapon-hung: grenades in silver filigree, electric batons curiously-wrought, the drone with beaked or dragon's face. We are wiser than to unleash these, rather feeding on the venom we secrete. When our hearts beat, they scream thug life. Yes, ever since that hour when we buried our angel, when we covered her with flowers and a sick rain fell in that open face and mad as a wood in winter we spread out over the land's slow waves: the naked, the twisted, the solitaries.

The wealth we seek is love, kinship, the house lit with joy; sorrow at our sides like a twin, a cowled advisor. We move along exile's spiralling trail, the thicket track, avoiding the bright avenues of the cold-at-soul, the gold-dazzled, the droolers after praise. We remember she who taught us, the feast of our union, the silenced transmissions from mind to delighted mind. Sometimes, our sorrow turned to sleep, we hold and kiss her radiant face, taking in our own paws those lithe and slender hands. And then to wake to the ruinous shore, the blonde-eyed seagull primping its whiteness, only the snow's caress! All our longings rise again as the vision redescends, snatched by memory's currents, sinking through the deeps. We have ridden down that wild sea's thread, and we are weary; the dead can speak, and we do not understand them.

The sacred, sentient, all-encompassing earth – this blissful infer-no, this blazing paradise, this pure bone-fire, this nether heaven – is the place where every scheme fails and falls. Can a man be thought wise until death itself has shaped his face? The loud mead-hall is in the ground with all its laughing voices. Dwelling on that, the dark mind reels. Hear, then, our warrior code: study patience; stay cool, fool; use a word with the same reluctance that you would a blade; see through the gleaming hoardings; move as though crossing a frozen river, as one who perceives his doom in each dilating cloud and each gesturing tree; identify your real en-emy; know happiness and sadness as figments of the mind; hold fast to the ancient ways; be gentle as the animals and a bastard when you must. We know that this swollen world's trillions will soon return to air, that the ivy's gleeful melody will play over glass and steel; buddleja on the runways, silence on the airwaves, these sleek and new-minted man-shells rusting in their mounds. And every soul now joined in breath having met its end alone: taken by the raven, asked by the grey wolf to dance, sent up the winding path to where the river springs. So they were destroyed before and will be again and again, the strongholds that we build to shutter out the light.

The contemplative, the self-taught, those who can cast a third eye over this Gotham globe, we do not forget the slain. *O my love, where are they, where are they going, I ask not in sorrow but wonder*. Where music once flowered is a wire-topped wall, the pace of black-clad mercenaries with peaked and snake-badged caps. Weapons thirst for blood, not men; once built, they will have their meat. Day falls, night rises, weird storm-clouds bloom. A winter readies its assault, ice prepares its curfew. The fatal sky will unpick the ties of enemies and friends, unbind the body's ligaments, unweave the banknote's cunning mesh and the very cloth of love. And we – hermits of the grim estates, exiles in our own domain, aristocrats of the wordless – set our feet in the igneous heavens and our sights on the holy ground.

TREMOR

One, reports said, rushed
from the room in terror,
was struck on the head

and instantly killed
by a lump of falling
masonry. Another, we heard,

dropped three floors
in a porcelain bath
to rest, regal, amongst

the smoking ruins,
amazed at her own
nakedness. And a third

was thrown (along with
his bed) into the open
arms of a tree, descended

into a new world.

3

The Sun

CLOUD

Such translucent seethe and coil
this architectural flow

self-weaving unweaving cobweb
wizard melting intricacy

wild celestial engine
revolving inward and outward now

moth-light beckoner
to the sun beneath the soil

imperial feathered gentlest strutting
over the stricken the rotten

disturbance in the ringing blue
desert of the mind

proceeding at the pace
of what we have forgotten

NATURE & ART

after Goethe

Though they seem to be different, Nature and Art –
if clearly seen – are a single growth.
Me, I no longer make the distinction;
seeking neither, I embody them both.
The whole arcanum's pure-minded intent,
the hours you give to the extinction
of all that's truly unintelligent
and blackens the tree that glows in the heart.

Such is the rule of self-cultivation:
they who imagine themselves to be free
may eyeball but never tread the white peak,
the far-shining pole of those who speak
of constraints that make a space for mastery.
To align with the Law's liberation.

MINING FOR BONE

A natural resource of my own,
this wealth of bone
below the skin,

this pale mineral
the blood has hoarded.
So far I have managed

only needles, idols,
have trudged through caves
where beasts were praised.

I'll persevere. I'll tunnel deep,
raise whole cities;
it is a rich seam.

ARLES

You arrive in February, the darkness
of Paris forgotten in the sheer light
of fresh snowfall, the black outlines of trees
like Japanese script in whitened gardens.
It is near, the strange harvest of your life.
You make a study of an old woman,

receive a visit from some friendly men
who also paint, are struck by the darkness
of the local girls, find somewhere to live.
By April, the damp orchards are alight –
they sign to you across broken gardens –
with the upraised flames of transfigured trees.

In September, you sit amongst the trees
and watch as a blank-faced man and woman
shuffle their way through the public gardens,
the blue firs bristling with lupine darkness.
You are able to take a child's delight
in everything, seeing it all alive

(innocent of your gimcrack afterlife,
the Vincent erasers and mousemat trees
arrayed in the giftshop's shadowless light).
Your business is the salvation of man,
to wash from our eagle eyes the darkness
that stops us knowing ourselves in the Garden,

that keeps us pacing the madhouse garden.
You paint the blaring sun, broadcasting live
from the galaxy's wild hub of darkness.
You are drawn to the cypresses, those trees
whose ominous figures resemble men
in their spiralling journey up to light.

You write of the 'blue depth' where the starlight
coils, of the jewels of that high garden;
you show no sign of the desperate man
who will voice the desire not to live,
illuminating this place of trees
where all's defined by a sinuous darkness.

*

When old men die, you said, they go on foot to light
from the darkness of these gardens.
We learn how to live by watching the trees.

THE SUN

after Baudelaire

Scattered papers wheel through streets where behind the boards
nailed to concrete hovels are lowlifes getting high,
at the hour when the original redoubles
on slate and wheat alike the rage of his beams;
there's me, alone again, a mental samurai
who scents in the shadows the echoing of words
or stumbles against them as over loose cobbles
or poems preconceived in childhood's monstrous dreams.

The enemy of sickliness, He who provides,
makes images and roses open at a touch;
dissolving sorrows like the white ships of the sky,
he sweetens brain and hive with golden roubles
and greens the withered cripple on the trunk of his crutch;
he gives to each thing such unburdened blood it seems
a laughing girl, his decree that all souls bud and fly
in the supreme heart where endless Aprils sing;
and when, poet-like, he bathes in city crowds
it's all that you'd call filth that he ennobles,
entering in turn as an incognito king
the mansions with their piled silence, the locked ward with its screams.

CUTTING CLASS

We slip by the brick estates
patterned like a lizard's back,

then suburbs where the conifer's
black flames stand sentinel;

we pass the clipped, uncanny gardens,
pace through the witchcraft

of the giant leaves of planes,
wade against the smoking tide

of insect-faced and swollen cars.
We skirt the sewage works,

cross over the motorway's grey
cortege to the dark

matter of the countryside –
Egypt's pylons scanning the fields,

evil spores in the undergrowth,
antennae needling the clouds –

and we just keep on toiling away
from town, setting our sights

on the grace and madness
of burning trees, as far as where

the truant woods dance
in a light that is breaking all the rules,

to the point at which we start to learn
to stand inside the fire.

The mark of the human is twofold, and consists in his or her relation to both language and the world. Concerning the latter it could be said that a human is one able to experience things at first hand, to *see* the black claws and the silvery shin where others only think 'a twig'. This encounter is more terrible than picturesque, more ignorant than knowing; its absence gives us literature. As regards language, the human's oddness consists simply in a heightened feeling for rhythm and an instinct for the precise – which is to say primordial – word.

A human is just a creature with an unusual capacity for astonishment, and the ability to utter that astonishment in speech that makes no sound.

DARK GREEN

Write this in whiter words but go forth on...
LIBER XXXI

Roars scrawl the night like white words on black paper,
An insect prays aloud, the rainbow anaconda
Illuminates the river as the trembling agouti
Nuzzles a brazil nut in its root-beamed den.

Far from the forest and the flame in each leaf
Other lives go on or seem to, ambling solo
Round sunlit parks filthy with talk and beer;
Each soul forgetting that the green dark holds us, how we
Stumble over its panthers in our sleep, love's
Touch as wildly silent as a blue-feathered dart.

RETURN

after Jules Laforgue

Earth places History in her deep coat:
farewell, holy and unholy mornings!
Buildings quiver? She merely clears her throat,
a fat lady getting ready to sing.
When you stagger, squinting, from the last night-
club, heads possessed by the last mad anthem,
the beaches are bleak as a used condom.
Children, return to the city of light.

Enough of this ocean whose dismal laugh
has driven the coastlines to breaking point;
an end to the wind that chews your ear off,
to that lame, interminable complaint.
Beneath the grey coffin lid of the skies
you've weathered rain with less wit than Noah,
but the time for misery is over.
Children, return to the city of light.

The strange craft of your flesh can take you there.
Somewhere ahead, the wild metropolis
is fatal, melodious, lucid, foursquare.
You will feel your way to the palaces
that have stood untenanted time out of mind,
throw open the shutters, raise the dust;
you have moped in the country long enough.
Children, return to the city of light.

*

Your sleeping forms are not less than divine.
Awaken, amnesiac magicians:
you are gods, take up your true positions.
Children, return to the city of light.

4

Where We Are the Dead

ANTIMIMON

O frondens virga

O greening branch! You stand in your nobility
like the inconceivable inmate of a star:

rejoice, exult and deign to free the fools we are
from the bright shade of the feigned tree of mystery.

Like the inconceivable inmates of a star,
shining with the rising dawn's calm velocity

through the bright shade of the feigned tree of mystery
where artificers play and none know who they are,

we rise with the shining dawn's calm velocity
to nibble on the paper leavings of a star.

The artificial lights, no one guesses what they are
and the drugged soul is the true atrocity,

rising to be eaten by a paper-grimaced star.
The bloomed car flames with the soul's ferocity

but the captured soul is the one atrocity,
not seeing the bough's *come join the grace that you are*.

The bloomed car blazes with its sole ferocity
upon the ailing slaves, the city's brightest star,

no one seeing its *come join the grace that you are*
conveyed in a gesture that is all charity;

above the limping slaves, the city's lightest star –
O greening branch! – you stand in your nobility,

saying with a gesture that all is charity:
rejoicing, exulting, freeing the fools we are.

FAKE NEWS FROM NOWHERE

We cannot *begin* the prison-break
without first convincing our fellow inmates

that they are in a prison at all;
they are incredulous, saying one eats

well on either sausage or steak,
pointing to the forest painted on the wall.

DRONES

You see the Greys, he said, girding his teeth
for a lime doughnut, they use the owl's
nervous system the way we use a drone
or hidden camera. Given what I now knew,
it almost seemed possible. When green tea
was announced I slid outside for a smoke,

paced roided grass, watched where stained smokestacks smoked
into the wind's dead breath, its yellow teeth.
Back in the conference centre, the tea-
fresh crowd were pondering the giant owl
that stilled her car on that night when she knew
she knew nothing, its voice a savage drone

terrible to recall, a rising drone
which turned her body into pixel-smoke
swarming upwards and assembled anew
('like I'd been sucked into a white hole's teeth')
on that craft that swept as quiet as an owl.
When she arrived home, hours late for tea,

her forehead was marked with a tau cross: T.
She paused, and the air conditioning's drone
momentarily quickened the cased owl
on the wall, living eyes long gone to smoke,
and shivered through the symmetrical teeth
of love's lost children (tell us something new!)

who'd come here to share what little they knew.
I thought of the onset of DMT –
that sense of deliverance into the teeth
of a buzzing gleam or luminous drone,
mere seconds after releasing the smoke –
and then of that line from *Twin Peaks*, 'the owls

are not what they seem'. I dozed, dreamt of owls
sane and inviolate in all they knew,
and awoke to the guest lecturer: *Smoke
and Mirrors, Carl Jung and the Abductee.*
With his grey skin, dark clothes and soothing drone
he might have been a priest. I licked furred teeth

clean of dough, grabbed a smoke with my teeth
and headed to where I knew mowers droned.
Love is an owl and it's having you for tea.

JUNGLIST

And, at its greatest intensity, it is as if
the insane din were in reality the profoundest of silences.
WALTER F. OTTO, *DIONYSUS: MYTH AND CULT*

To raze the mind is the drums' one desire.
They chant, in darkness, that light is a grave.
Their speech is the speech of shadow and fire.

Some flicker softly like moths in a jar
but mostly they sing a mechanical rage.
To raze the mind is the drums' one desire.

We hear them at night, for now from afar,
but picture the woods, the dance and the blaze
where speech is the speech of shadow and fire.

They drum from within, each tap of the heart
disturbing thought and these orderly days.
To raze the mind is the drums' one desire.

We hear drums bellow, the earth stands ajar
and all its passionate creatures gape:
their speech is the speech of shadow and fire.

Sometimes a frenzy will summon such quiet;
sometimes a rhythm can sound like a fate.
To raze the mind is the drums' one desire.
Their speech is the speech of shadow and fire.

MATRIX

i Vista

Our sole legacy,
splintered plastic toys litter
the castle precincts.

ii Vernal

In truth, winter won.
The beauty of this season's
mere apparition.

iii Untitled

He is nobody,
he is unafraid. At dawn,
deep in the gardens.

MUSED

Chinoiserie of the turbulence –
her guys didn't call it crystalline
for nothing – and the suspended dance
of the shore's cedar-spelled depths, the nine
miles of dark light between town and town
where the machine of our thought relents
and you see that you are on your own
with this grace that peoples the silence;

on your own but for something that hunts
and sends through the trees a clear glass sound,
a call that scans, such eerie parlance.
It was unwise not to bring your hound.
The frozen air rings, no earthly bell,

shaping in you a deer's vigilance;
you want to live, to sing; you flee, all
patterned over with sweet arguments.

REIGN

after Verlaine

I used to dream of metaphysical bling
and Persian or papal sumptuosity,
of Sardanapalus and Elagabalus;
I raised with sheer desire a star-tiled ceiling
sustained on the scent of silent melody:
the spiritual joy of the flesh's endlessness.

Calmer today though hungrier, while
perceiving that true wisdom is to move panther-style,
I loose my madness by reining it in
without one note of surrender in my pace.
So what if the infinite outstrips me at times?
Consign the pleasant to the bargain bin!
God how I despise the presentable face,
the once-daring friend and all credulous rhymes.

WAKING

for Mark Blanco

At the edge of the woods, where reality bites.
At the edge of the woods, with the listening pines.
At the edge of the woods, where a black bird laughs.
At the edge of the woods, where the moss is alight.
At the edge of the woods, where the grasshopper strolls.
At the edge of the woods, where small leaves roar.
At the edge of the woods, where the wind's a caress.
At the edge of the woods, where thickets cavort.
At the edge of the woods, where the sun bears down.
At the edge of the woods, where the heart is stronger.
At the edge of the woods, where the land is electric.
At the edge of the woods, where everything talks.
At the edge of the woods, where sobriety plays.
At the edge of the woods, where vision is X-ray.
At the edge of the woods, where tales are recalled.
At the edge of the woods, where light is a searchlight.
At the edge of the woods, where the Stone Age shines.
At the edge of the woods, where the wood's camouflaged.
At the edge of the woods, where the twigs touch the light.
At the edge of the woods, where geometry grows.
At the edge of the woods, in the Gothic era.
At the edge of the woods, where the children are lost.
At the edge of the woods, with the fire salamander.
At the edge of the woods, in the mind's Alhambra.
At the edge of the woods, where the path is no path.
At the edge of the woods, where the wire is barbed.
At the edge of the woods, where an oak weighs the sun.
At the edge of the woods, where the wood is a dance.
At the edge of the woods, where the mind will roost.
At the edge of the woods, where the pattern is clear.
At the edge of the woods, where eyes are ears.
At the edge of the woods, where the heart is a child.

At the edge of the woods, in an autumnal light.
At the edge of the woods, where a shout gives no sound.
At the edge of the woods, where our hands are empty.
At the edge of the woods, where love has no mercy.
At the edge of the woods, where the fungus gloats.
At the edge of the woods, where teeth are stones.
At the edge of the woods, where the grass is at home.
At the edge of the woods, when you're so far from home.
At the edge of the woods, where the wolf's everywhere.
At the edge of the woods, in the unending stare.
At the edge of the woods, where the water is deep.
At the edge of the woods, where the wood knows nothing.
At the edge of the woods, where trees are melodies.
At the edge of the woods, where we eat red berries.
At the edge of the woods, where crickets chant.
At the edge of the woods, where there's nowhere to turn.
At the edge of the woods, when you know where to turn.
At the edge of the woods, in a still Bacchanal.
At the edge of the woods, where the dead hold hands.
At the edge of the woods, where we are the dead.
At the edge of the woods, in the wood's arabesques.
At the edge of the woods, where rain is impending.
At the edge of the woods, where pride will crouch.
At the edge of the woods, where the heart howls.
At the edge of the woods, where silence is golden.
At the edge of the woods, where her face gives light.
At the edge of the woods, where the ink's on our hands.
At the edge of the woods, where tongues are gentle.
At the edge of the woods, where knowledge is weeping.
At the edge of the woods, where the skeleton sings.
At the edge of the woods, where the woods will eat us.
At the edge of the woods, where thistles preen.
At the edge of the woods, where trees are feathers.
At the edge of the woods, where it goes up in smoke.
At the edge of the woods, when our watches slow.
At the edge of the woods, where the drone is of flies.

At the edge of the woods, where the news is of silence.
At the edge of the woods, where the clouds are webs.
At the edge of the woods, where the sky's full of spiders.
At the edge of the woods, when the game is over.
At the edge of the woods, *in excelsis gloria*.
At the edge of the woods, when the dragon flies.
At the edge of the woods, where the gold is mined.
At the edge of the woods, where the flies rub their hands.
At the edge of the woods, where it all comes to mind.
At the edge of the woods, where the words are faded.
At the edge of the woods, where we are the hunted.
At the edge of the woods, where we're wise as snakes.
At the edge of the woods, where the mind will wander.
At the edge of the woods, where the woods are the answer.
At the edge of the woods, where Rip van Winkle sleeps.
At the edge of the woods, where the day shows its bones.
At the edge of the woods, where the modest rose.
At the edge of the woods, where you watch your step.
At the edge of the woods, where we speak the argot.
At the edge of the woods, where it goes without saying.
At the edge of the woods, where we're only beginning.
At the edge of the woods, where our sons go to war.
At the edge of the woods, where the woods never end.
At the edge of the woods, when the world is turning.
At the edge of the woods, where you bite on the bullet.
At the edge of the woods, where the woods are perfect.
At the edge of the woods, where bodies are waking.
At the edge of the woods, where a branch taps your back.
At the edge of the woods, in the silent bonfire.
At the edge of the woods, the whole shooting match.

ONE BELOW

The frost is an epoch that will not last
the land for this one day one vast white coast
a single branch where the ice fowls roost
each perfectly empty tree its own wild ghost

5

Flagrant Stamen

ROOMS

When thirty spokes put their heads together
or clay is coaxed into a form and baked,
you have a wheel that flashes round a hole
and a pot whose treasure is an empty space;

we raise a roof and four solid walls
to build a house but we occupy the air;
our being in the world depends upon
mastering the use of what isn't there.

(Tao Te Ching vi)

WHEEL RIVER

after Wang Wei

i

We have made our residence on the brink,
where the willow is living and dying.
Grave scholars who read us will never think
that the dead inherit everything.

ii

Birds take themselves off into the stillness.
October glows as if painted on glass.
I stroll up the hill with my loneliness,
secure in the knowledge that nothing lasts.

iii

The hazel's lichen-freaked trunks are my walls.
My great leaf-roof whispers God's hundredth name.
Alive in the woods, I cook up a storm
that will whirl to the cities. A real rain.

iv

Arterial trees reflecting in waters
hang downwards, suspended over a void:
we are dark heaven's thin sons and daughters,
rooted in soil we strive to avoid.

v

Country so deserted it seems crowded.
The lack of conversation fills my days.
In the shady depth of the mothering glen
are moss hairs lit by the sun's close gaze.

vi

The day gives the crisped hills a last caress.
A skein of geese undulates through the sky.
Here and there, an evergreen like a fire.
The clouds descend but find no place to rest.

vii

Come visit me. It's psilocybin time;
the brambles hold their black constellations.
We can groan in night-long ruminations,
getting 'lost in the unknown, famous light'.

viii

In the tunnel of this overhung path
the starred moss deepens its luminous pile.
I pick up every stone I see, while
there's still a chance some pretty feet might pass.

ix

I dream I am sailing into the sky.
The clouds clear and another Earth is there,
a pavilion where we sit together.
We can hear nothing but the butterflies.

x

Satellites scan the world's inhuman shores.
The mind's antipodes are still unknown,
but no boat will make that crossing. Alone,
you must step into the sea-monster's jaws.

xi

A melody blows us over the lake.
We call goodbye in the growing dark.
When I turn, the clouds have a dragon's face.
Entirety smoulders in every part.

xii

At the palace, the pavements and coiffeured trees
would quickly drive me to despair. Out here,
I stray through a withered chaos of leaves
where everything's in perfect order.

xiii

Streamlets like schoolchildren hurry down rocks,
the rain spits in my face, the bare wind sings
something I can't catch. In a dream, I watch
white egrets ascending and descending.

xiv

You can take your monatomic gold,
your organic wheatgrass (locally sourced!),
your chicken soup for the insatiable soul.
To live forever, just drink from the source.

xv

Another dream: I'm with Walt Whitman,
we are standing in a broad stream's shallows.
His ankles pale, that loneliest of men
is telling me the secret names of the stones.

xvi

An object hums above the forest,
a shining sphere with no rivets or seams.
When I come to my senses, my mind clean,
I find I can't account for several minutes.

xvii

Compose in darkness: yes. These eyes are clear
enough to discern a world's death-rattle.
I'm so far out, I'd be invisible
was it not for the moon's closed-circuit stare.

xviii

I think of Chuang Tzu, the idiot's post
that was the only job he ever had;
he fields another call, keeping a tab
on the tragic gestures of the willows.

ixx

In late December, the wrecked wood flowers.
Everything opens, unfurls its light
in the disused mansion at the river's side:
our strange faces, the tips of our fingers.

We have emptied these hands and cupped our minds,
made a salad from the garden's choicest leaves,
left milk in saucers, tasted the breeze,
hailed the thunder. Now let the lightning strike.

NOTE Wang Wei (699–761), a contemporary of the better-known Li Po and Tu Fu, was in his lifetime as celebrated for his paintings as for his poetry. He had a successful career as a court official, yet after the deaths of his wife and mother spent increasing periods in the solitude of his Wang River estate (*wang*, literally 'wheel rim'). This remake of his famous sequence of short poems was an experiment in what might be termed hieroglyphic translation (by hieroglyphic I refer to the true function of sacred writing, whereby an image and its associations are allowed to resound in the mind – centrifugally but not arbitrarily – like the ripples of a stone thrown into a still pond). An occasional literary or cinematic allusion parallels the typical T'ang incorporation of fragments of classic poems, songs or chants, the one explicit borrowing being from Dylan Thomas's 'Poem on His Birthday'.

SAYS

A truth's a thing that will not disappear.
I have the queen bee inside my right ear.

RELIC

after Guilhèm de Peitieus

I'm not going to chat no shit no more
these skewed lines aren't either about you or
the Sacred Heart or those who adore
Grand Theft Auto's incidents
and in any case I write as I sit and snore
on the fence

I don't know when or where or what I'll be born
I can see into the dark and I'm blinded by the dawn
I'm like an Ethiopian called Bjorn
I'm unbearably tense
since one white night my aura was torn
upon an eminence

I don't know if I'm up or lucid dreaming
my days are lagging when they should be streaming
an infected mind's less loving than scheming
lives by pretence
and hides itself in the ranks of the seeming
ladies and gents

I'm sick but I'm scared of the touch of death
and all I can hear is the TV's breath
and my mouth is a state yet I don't slam meth
and I've the sense
that nowadays everyone's a dosed Macbeth
wishing their end would commence

I've my soulmate by my side though I don't know her well
she's rarer than words though there's little to tell
my indifference if she held me or gave me hell
would be immense

though I wonder what it would take to dispel
her silence

She's the world to me but I've never seen her face
and I never gave her cause to spray me with mace
and when she's distant I proceed apace
through a dense
crowd of beauties whose fingers' knowing grace
is a gentle violence

I've said what I swore not to concerning the unknown
person I speak for who'll sing it alone
and ponder and place it under a stone
for the elements
a skeleton key a rainmaking bone
produced at my own expense

GOA

Wahr spricht wer Schatten spricht

It was our eyes
that were broken:
the palm tree's face,
swayed by the night

it shadows forth,
is without flaw.
It was reason
that dreamed, that dreams:

the surf intent
(this one moment
of the world's end)
as thin white wolves,

lithe hordes licking
the fortress walls.
It was the news
that kept us old;

the webbed sky teems
with unseen fleets,
each unloved stone
love's nameless hue

in the golden
links of your paw,
full of the dark
speech that speaks true.

TWIN PEAKS

after Li Po

We come into the heights in search of you
and see ourselves, dogs barking at a stream
whose splashes deepen the flower's deep blue.

Is this real or some strange and twisted dream?

In the silence of the unlifted bell
black trees splay bony fingers above us,
the crag-hanging torrents forget to fall.

Noon. *Do not sing. The world is perfect. Hush!*

An old man I question looks right through me;
in the shadows, an antlered gaze meets mine.
Too tired to think, I lean against a pine.

Soundless laughter permeates the valleys.

TO CATCH A THIEF

You've been dead a generation and yet there you are still,
poised and serene and barely more than twenty,
divine, unattainable.

Incomparable Grace, you marry a prince and grow old.
When I ride in pursuit of the enemy,
though, it's your face on my shield.

SELF-PORTRAIT AS T'ANG POET AT DUSK

This far from the city one bears no unearthly toy
there's nothing now here or in heaven that does not fly
the blue air's shining lamentations are somehow joy

I'm a domestic terrorist a walking thoughtcrime
I'm a coin through whose square pupil you can see the sky
from my star-domed terrace I watch the slow dance of time

a day is the merest gauze in which the night is dressed
what need of many books when I have love's live ember
the world is always waving like a departing guest

the waterfall's catastrophe radiates its white
each ghost-drawn tree's the ideogram for Remember
the unspeakableness of all this is why I write

marvelling how the light can darken and still be light

VOYAGER

The little Love-god lying once asleep…

Let me beam you a song that is the song
of you all, a true story of a cruise as long
as its horror is real and which I still endure,
the red blink of my heart the one thing sure
in this utter ocean as black as it is ice;
of this freight of golden howls, the frail device
of my face parting the tides of the sun
on the endless night-watch, the towering
cliffs of birdless islands revolving past my wing
and my tin feet bathed in the absolute zero
of their wake, an automatic sorrow
running through the circuits of my sea-eaten brain.
The man still inside the blessings of the rain –
fine earth underfoot, a daughter or son

trailing behind and then darting ahead –
cannot conceive of those currents I've rode, those dead
winter surges of my shaken trajectory,
the frost that patterns me like a story
chiselled on the tomb of a navigating king;
and nothing to hear but the void pulsating,
the ever-vacant whirr, the ringed orb's drone,
an iron silence in which no gull praised
branching wave and branching light, no curlew amazed
the humming mind awake with its ghost of a cry
(but I have their records stored like wines, I
guard their lyrics like the dead's delighted laughter),
not one note perched on that echoed hall's rafter
where I sailed on through its mansions of bone.

What I did hear, in the permanent roar
of the standing hexagon on Saturn's north shore,

82

was a shriek as of a wraith with metal feathers
nitrogen-dewed, vast inclement weathers
radiating outwards like haze that taints the sky;
but none to share the vision, no hand close by
with that shining ratio love unfolds
or its sweet kinship of divine disdain,
far as I was from you who have to dose the pain
of crowded solitude by tricking out your cells
with mimic love and light (those broadcast spells,
intoxicants all); alone I trace the dark,
the paths of night, no companionable ark
but the sole witness of what my craft beholds

on the mean streets of this high sea. Shadows
lose substance as the sun recedes, iced methane snows
on Titan, down the unavailing space-grit rains
like someone is sowing porcelain grains;
my dials tremble with an exile's vertigo,
quake between joy and terror, wild to go
with the towering stream of the central tree
that waves like an ash on a day of storm,
to be sucked along those entwined boughs to the warm
airs and opening worlds of a bird-minded race
(just as no man's so at home in his face,
so deep in the arms of his darling one
that he does not sweat at the thought of the One
and his lonely flight to the Alone, the mystery,

that he's never struck by music's silence
or the blank in the gaze of so-called science
or the immateriality of that and this
or the absence in the depth of a kiss,
conceiving instead a thirst for the furthest shore).
I think of your ascendant woods lit once more,
of leafing spires in the vague city's maze
and a bright green spire where mantises pray;

I think of those whose minds will discover the way
to the land's brink, that tangled footpath to the stars
you climb with closed eyes through the sky's briars,
the returning track of which the sure bird sings
when its plain song summons inexpressible things
perched on the border of your nights and days.

Such ones will seem odd to all whose sense
of what is and isn't real is hijacked by events
narrated on the airwaves, each new fearfest
drumming home the point that home's where you're safest;
in the room's corner, where a live fire should inform,
a digital flicker keeps nobody warm.
But now my warbling heart (*wirbil*, 'whirlwind')
spins beyond its case to remotely view
that open prison I have left, the whale-psalmed blue,
the great curving routes of the migratory spheres
and the turbulence of their atmospheres,
then comes back with a vast screech of admonition:
forget your readings and forget your mission,
keep on and don't look back until you find

joys holier than that pen where life means death
can give you, that paradise where a dragon's breath
rusts the fruit on the branch and the coin in your hand,
that demon-sucked and pestilential land
where disease is a business and health is a loss,
where youth is bent, where a sword can reach across
a hemisphere to gut an ambling man
and sharp-eyed spears drift at the edge of space;
and, truly, a warrior who would gain his place
amongst the angels, they who sing the raging calm,
must take his stand against the ring-fenced farm –
if he cares to fight for the living epitaph
of his great-great-granddaughter's unenslaved laugh –
where the meat and milk and blood is human.

The sunlight is veiled, the empires it grew
looted and labelled, the king's jewelled retinue
scattered, his exploits a stele that none can translate;
and no gold to give that is not gold plate,
no exulting heroes but smooth-voiced snakes in suits
('strategic consultants', the mind that computes)
who blanch beneath a diplomatic smile;
and the letters of Nature's sacred book
unillumined in the eyes of those too dazed to look,
the drained men a premature senility
curls up like leaves; and in that grey city,
behind a brace of code-locked doors, a lord who trusts
in his wealth – Selah *– yet secretly lusts*
for a body that death might never defile

grows pale at the thought of his failing strength
and all those proud forebears tuned to the grave's wavelength,
for a name's not a house that the storm won't lay bare
and you can't buy grace with a silver prayer –
hear me open my dark saying *– and piles of gold*
won't make that strange chamber one degree less cold,
recalling the wages of monstrous greed.
Wondrous the one who flows in His stillness,
embodies the bedrock, whose breath is the clearness
of the world-spangled heavens and the lichened wood,
and blessed are those who live simply – not 'good',
but listening less to the talk than the thunder –
and lost is the herd with no sense of wonder
(he who thinks he knows is a fool indeed,

not once having died while still drawing breath:
'Almighty God, what is this? My boy, this is death').
To recognise the Word which glows in every stone
is to feel your flesh grow light, is to own
nothing but that wild and tender sense of creaturehood,
is to step gently, it being understood

that the way is a way of restraint;
an outer and an inner cleanliness
becomes the pupil – Hugiaine! – who judges less
than he suffers with all those who moan in their sleep,
clear in enmity as he is in deep
love, casting no man in the hieroglyphic fire
before his time, knowing His code is higher
and wider than conception can paint

or poem build. Let no soul succumb
to deceit but consider what it has become
and what it is, a child of the star-toned origin
all things point to and where they rebegin,
and why and how it is obstructed from seeing
that radiance that is the body's being,
the birthright of whole-eyed women and men
upright on the earth. Praise to the One
and to the Holy Mother Spirit and the Son,
Christos and Sophia – words that believe in silence
and She who is the light of that immense
and waking garden – and courage to the fool
who holds the flagrant stamen these waters cannot cool,
now and forever. Onwards. Amen.

*